Next Steps

Dr. Lamar T. Collins

Printed in the United States of America
Published: by Legacy Voice Productions

Cover Design & Sketch By

Yasir Nadeem & Vince White

ISBN: 979-8-9856062-9-4

To contact author for booking or ordering
additional copies, go to:
drltcollins18@gmail.com

Dedication

Let me start by saying that I'm a very fortunate man. I married a woman that supports me wholeheartedly and unconditionally. Although I've made many mistakes, she is always there to help me through my hang ups. Rose Collins, I can't thank you enough for your love and support.

I also want to thank the many mentors I've had that have pushed me during my career, including Loria Lofton, Paul Englekirk, Cliffa Foster, Tony Evans, Bishop Lawrence Windom, Bishop John Tolbert, Bobby Ott, Todd Cutler and many more.

Finally, I want to thank the speakers, authors, and businesspersons that have developed material that has aided my personal growth and development. This list includes, but isn't limited to Creflo Dollar, Colin Powell, Tony Robbins, Claude Anderson, Thomas Sowell, J.C Watts, Cornell West, Dennis Kimbro, John Maxwell, Malcolm Gladwell, and Stephen Covey.

Next Steps

This book is designed for those who are just finishing one chapter of life and moving to another. Specifically, those of you moving to a new level of responsibility, leadership, or opportunity. You may have just finished high school, college, trade school, or just gotten out of the military. Maybe you just finished medical school, graduated from the academy, or received a promotion. Maybe you just got out of prison and you're ready to be a productive member of society. Many are congratulating you, patting you on the back, and telling you what a good job you've done to get to where you are. Well, I wrote this book to bring you back to earth. You may think you've made it past the hard part, but the truth is you haven't experienced the hard part yet. I know people are telling you that

you've accomplished a great feat but allow me to burst that bubble--you haven't done anything yet. Don't get me wrong, I do want you to enjoy yourself for a little while… a very little while. Take a deep breath, look at yourself in the mirror and smile, hang your diploma on the wall—and then get back to work, because it's time to make a difference. Listen, I know some people are already turned off and wonder why someone would give you a book like this but let me tell you why.
Your success in one chapter of life prepares you for but doesn't guarantee success in the next chapter of life. This chapter will be full of changes and quick decisions, and I've written this book to help you prepare for these decisions.

Think about light rays. When light is scattered (when the sun is shining) its power is limited; however, when light energy is focused (a laser beam), it can cut through metal. Let's consider water. Those tiny water drops cause little problems by themselves, but when water molecules work together in a focused effort, the aftermath, such as a tsunami or hurricane unleashes a tremendous amount of power.
The purpose of this book is to challenge you to focus on a few areas of life. Five to be exact. If you are going to unlock the greatness that is in you and make it to the next level of success, it is going to take a focused effort. I know you just went through a lot to get to where you are now, but that was about you. Now it's time to focus your energy and efforts so that you might make

a meaningful difference in society. The goal is not to simply be successful. The goal is to live a life of significance. The goal is not simply to have enough to provide for you and your family. The goal is to make a difference in someone else's life that will change their very existence. To do this it takes more than making a decision to be great. Trust me, that's the easy part. After we make the decision to strive for greatness, we have to manage the decision we just made. Decision managing is so much more important than decision making. If you are not in agreement so far, give this book to someone else because I'm not talking to you. However, if you feel what I'm saying pull up your bootstraps. Cut off the television for a few evenings and invest in reading this short but powerful book.

As I said, there are five areas in which I want to challenge you to focus. I believe that if you prioritize these five areas, you will not only achieve personal success, but you will also be (in part) responsible for the success of many others. And that my friend, in my opinion is why we are here. We are here to bless and benefit others through our own unique blend of gifts, talents and abilities.

Here are the five areas we will delve into:

1. <u>Discover Your Strengths</u>- Understand
   your unique blend of gifts, talents, and
   abilities
2. <u>Develop Good Friendships</u>- Who you
   hang around determines who you
   become
3. <u>Decide to Maintain a Positive Attitude</u>-
   Attitude moreso than aptitude
   ultimately determines altitude
4. <u>Discipline Yourself</u>- You will become
   what you are becoming
5. <u>Discern Life's Plan</u>- No one can do what you
   have been called to do. If you don't do it, the
   world will go lacking.

I am sure you have already given thought and
intentional effort to these five areas. You
would not be where you are if you had not.
However, please allow me to stretch
your thinking a little.

Discover Your Strengths

If you is who you aint, then you aint who you is... and if you're not who you should be, you'll never be who you could be-- old proverb

The first thing I want to challenge you to focus on is developing your strengths. You see, we all have a unique blend of gifts, talents, and abilities. That is why you should never feel jealous of someone else (somebody just got delivered right there). Listen, so many people walk through life depressed because they know their weaknesses without knowing their strengths. The life changing question is not what I don't do well or why am I not as good as others. The life changing question is what do I do well? There are many things you don't do well, and that's okay. It's okay because there are also many things that you do well. Stop focusing on what your weaknesses are and start focusing on your strengths.

Real success in life will never come by focusing on weaknesses, so stop it! We live in a day when everyone wants to be the best. Consider that for a moment. If the only way to be happy is to be the best, then only one person/group can really be happy, because only one can be the best.
Let's consider a track meet. There are only a select few athletes focused on setting a world record (meaning they are the best).

What do most track coaches ask athletes to focus
on? Track coaches ask athletes to focus on setting
personal records. The goal is not to be better than
everyone else. The goal is to be better than you've
ever been. You are not running life's race to
be better than someone else. You are running life's
race to constantly outperform your prior efforts. So,
instead of trying to be better than everyone else,
focus on being the best version of you that you can
be.

Our society places way too much emphasis on
accomplishment and not nearly enough emphasis on
giving maximum effort, which is the absolute best
you can do. I once heard 5-time NBA champion
Kobe Bryant say a key to being a champion is to
challenge your potential. In other words, continue to
push yourself out of your comfort zone in the
area of your strengths. That is how you maximize
your potential, by focusing on and challenging
yourself in the area of your strengths. Not by
sulking over the inadequacies of your weaknesses.

No, you didn't make first chair, no you're not going
to be the starter, and no you didn't win the award…
so what! The real question is did you do your best.
If you did, feel good about yourself. If you didn't,
get busy!!!! Let me close this portion by saying
even in your strength area, you may not be the best.
It's not always about you having the best
performance. It's about the results. How do you
make people feel when you operate in your strength

zone? How do you influence and impact others? That's way more important than the final score.

Author and speaker Malcolm Gladwell discusses the 10,000-hour rule in his book outliers. His point is that to become really good at something, it takes about 10,000 hours of meaningful, purposeful practice. This theory was developed through observing Olympic athletes, singing groups (Beatles), and other successful individuals (ex. Bill Gates).

Work is not a dirty word. Everybody will eventually work hard or suffer the consequences. My suggestion is to find an area of giftedness that you possess and enjoy, and spend countless hours developing yourself in that area, whether you are the best or not. Are people blessed and benefited by your influence and impact? Life is a team sport and if you're going to win, you have to surround yourself with people operating in their strength, while you are operating in your strength. The team that wins the championship is not always the team with the best players. It is the team with the best players that maximize their strengths in a given system consistently over time. Identify who's on your team and whose team you're on; work together (collaborate) to maximize each other's potential and watch success follow. Remember, if you take the easy way out, life becomes hard. If you accept the challenge, life becomes easier.

Character

Before I move forward, I have to take a step back. I want you to focus on your strengths when it comes to your giftedness. If you can't sing well, I wouldn't advise you to focus on becoming an award-winning singer, because it probably won't happen. Character, however, is another subject. When it comes to character, appreciate your strengths, but focus on your weaknesses. You see, we can all be men and women of great character. You may have gotten this far with character flaws, but trust me, they will eventually catch up with you. It is important to acknowledge your character flaws.

You know what they are. Stop telling yourself, "That's just the way I am." That's your problem, that's the way you are. Acknowledge them and develop a plan to overcome them. Sometimes this takes outside intervention. It doesn't make you any less of a man or woman to admit that you have issues that are difficult for you to deal with. Consider this if a child is born with a speech impediment, they go to a speech therapist. If a person gets into an accident and is left with physical challenges, they see a physical therapist. So why is there a problem if a person is born with or develops mental or emotional challenges sees a counselor, psychologist, or psychiatrist? It isn't a problem.

Here's a secret. We all have issues for which we need help. The time for allowing the issue to manifest as a character flaw is over. Find an accountability partner or counselor if necessary. A support group, spiritual mentor, or someone to walk with you through your character challenge. It has always amazed me how easy it seems to discount emotional or mental challenges. They should be addressed just as physical challenges are. We prescribe therapy and rehab for physical challenges. I submit to you the same is needed for some emotional/mental challenges.

What separates humans from other organisms is that we have the ability to modify our behavior. Birds will always fly south for the winter, salmons will always swim upstream to give birth to their young, and pigs will always run for the mud, but humans are different. We have complex brains with the capacity to think and change. I'm not saying change is easy, I'm saying it's possible. A friend once told me that the only person that doesn't mind change is a wet baby. There is much truth to that statement, but it's also true that our greatness is in our willingness to change. In fact, change is a sign of growth. If something is growing, it is changing. Think about it, babies grow physically, their diet changes, their vocabulary changes, eventually their dress changes. There should come a point in time when our mentality, attitude, and character changes. The ability to change is a sign of maturity.

Identify areas in which you need to change and take action. Listen, you can't overcome what you don't identify, so identify the areas and develop a plan to attack your character weaknesses. Don't get mad at me, you know I'm right. I'm just telling you the truth. Some of you have acknowledged your weaknesses and for that I applaud you, but acknowledgement alone is not change. Change is not change when you recognize the need to change; change isn't change when you apologize and decide to change; "change is change when you change" (Creflo Dollar).

Talents

Talent is a different issue. When you identify the areas in which you excel, that's where your focus should go. I'm tone deaf, so why would I try to cut a music CD? When it comes to talents, focus on your strengths. If you are good with your hands, begin looking at possible careers that will allow you to build or repair things with your hands. If you speak well and are articulate, maybe you should pursue a career as a television reporter.

On a scale of 1-10, what are you naturally a 5 or 6 at? If you develop that, you could become an 8, 9, or 10. 8's, 9's, and 10's get compensated very well for the services they render. On the contrary, if you are naturally a 3 or 4 at something and you develop into 5 or 6, you're still barely average. Being average does not pay well nor does it make a significant difference. That's why you should strive to develop your strengths, the things at which you are already good. That is where you will make the biggest difference.

Let's look at it this way. How do you define success? Think about it, what does success mean to you. Is it how much you acquire? Is it how much you acquire compared to someone else? Here's a secret, if your success is based on money or material possessions, it'll never be enough. There will always be an upgrade or a newer model. If it's based on outperforming someone else, your quest is fruitless as there will always be someone with more. Can I suggest that it's okay to be happy where you are with what you have? Realize that what you have is more than at least 75% of the people on the planet. You actually have everything you need. It may not be the brand you desire, but you really do have what you need.

You may desire a 4-bedroom house, but you'll actually sleep the same as you do in that 2-bedroom apartment. I know you want a 75" flat screen but watching the game won't be more exciting than it is on the 35". A 500 series BMW would be nice, but you'll get to work at the same time as you do in a Ford Fiesta. Get my point? Don't get so caught up

in wanting a bigger and better standard of
living that you fail to enjoy your current
quality of life. I'm not saying to become
complacent; I'm saying be content while
striving for more. Isn't it interesting how
many are conditioned to always be looking at
the next stage of life? So much so that they
fail to enjoy the current stage of life.

Consider this:
- In the teens, many just want to get
out of school
- In the 20's many want to get a
good job or start a family
- In the 30's many want their kids
to grow up and graduate
- In the 40's many want their kids
to become self-sufficient and start a
family
- In the 50's many want grandkids

- In the 60's it's retirement time!
- In the 70's you wake up and realize you've
spent your whole life focusing on where you're
going and forgot to enjoy the journey.

If you have relative health and meaningful
relationships, count yourself blessed. I do want
you to strive for more, but don't forget to
appreciate and enjoy where you are today. Success
is progressive. You can enjoy where you are while
striving for more.

Okay now, let's look at 3 definitions of
   success.

1) <u>The first definition of success is
   simply the accomplishment of a
   goal</u>. If you set a goal,
   and accomplish it, you are
   successful. This is why Colonel
   McCraven at a University of Texas
   commencement ceremony
   (YouTube it, you'll like it)
   encouraged the recent graduates to
   start their day by making up their
   beds. If you don't do anything else
   all day, at least you accomplished
   one thing. This is a cure for feeling
   like a failure. Set a goal,
   accomplish it
   and you will feel successful,
   because
   you are successful. Start small, then
    build to bigger things.

2) <u>The second definition of success is when
   preparation meets opportunity</u>. The
   opportunity to be successful is coming, that's
   undeniable. The question is will you be ready
   when it comes. You don't know when
   it's coming, but it is. That's why you can't
   waste time. If the opportunity comes and
   you're not ready, you'll miss it. That
   opportunity may not come around again for
   months or years.

In some cases, that opportunity might not come again. I am reminded of a football player that had a couple of encounters with the law. He had overcome many of his legal troubles and was about to sign a contract with the Kansas City Chiefs. He went before the judge one last time for what he thought would be probation. The judge sentenced him, and he never played in the NFL. It wasn't because he didn't have the ability. He made choices that caused him to forfeit the opportunity and it never came again.

Consider a person that takes 5 years to graduate college instead of 4. There were opportunities there at year 4 that might not be there in year 5. Furthermore, consider the money lost. The average college graduate makes about $40,000 per year. Instead of making $40,000 that year, she is still paying for college. The first year's salary is not the biggest calamity. The next year when she graduates, she will get $40,000. She got it late, but she got it. What she forfeited was her last year's salary, which will likely be much more than $40,000. If she works 25 years, remember, she will forfeit her last year's salary because it would have been 26 years if she had graduated a year earlier. She can never get that year back. It's not a stretch to assume her last year's salary would be close to $100,000 or more. By graduating a year later,

she didn't forfeit $40,000. She forfeited the
last salary of over $100,000, because that's the
salary she'll never get!

Consider the man wanting a promotion but is
not working towards it. Suddenly, his boss is
transferred, and the company needs
a replacement. He's not even considered
because he has not worked towards it. He now
has to wait until another position opens or the
new person leaves. How long will that take?
The time to start is now! One more example.
An athlete is a backup and doesn't really pay
attention in practice because he's not
expected to play. The starter gets hurt and he
is expected to come in and perform to
standard. He doesn't do well because he's
making mental mistakes due to lack of
preparation. You never know when your
opportunity is coming, so always prepare as if
it is coming tomorrow. Amazingly enough,
opportunities often find the well prepared.
Think for a second. How many opportunities
have you wasted because you weren't
prepared? Ouch.

3) <u>The third definition is fulfilling your life's
   purpose</u>. You weren't born to be another
   number or simply occupy space. You were
   born to make a difference. What difference
   were you born to make? You were born to
   fulfill a purpose. What's your purpose?
   Don't know- me either, but I do know the

first step is discovering your strengths. The
reason you have strengths in the areas you are
strong in is because they are aligned to your
purpose. So, stop feeling bad because you
weren't the starting quarterback and begin
realizing you are really good at fixing things,
at talking to people, at problem-solving. At
whatever! Your strengths are aligned to your
purpose.

What is it that comes naturally to you that
causes other people marvel? You don't even
recognize it as a great strength because it's
intuitive to you. You may even find yourself
getting angry at others because they're not as
good as you in that area and you don't
understand why. I'll tell you why, it's your
strength zone. Identify and develop it because
tomorrow's success depends on today's
development of those gifts. The question is
not are you gifted. The questions are, where
are your areas of giftedness and what are you
doing to develop them?

To further emphasize this point, let me tell
you a story about Mr. Duck. Mr. Duck went
to the sign in table for the Special Olympics
for animals. The man at the sign in table said
Mr. Duck, "what do you want to do, what do
you want to be?" About that time Mr. Duck
saw an eagle soaring in the sky. The eagle
was so high that Mr. Duck said I want to be
an eagle and I want to soar to the heights of

the sky. The man at the sign in table said,
"you know ducks don't make good eagles"
but in life you get to make your own choices
so the man at the sign in table said, "Mr.
Duck, have at it". Mr. Duck climbed the tree
and jumped out of the tree and started
flapping those wings but again ducks can't
soar like eagles. He started falling, he hit a
branch then he hit the side of the tree, then he
hit another branch and boom! He fell to the
ground. He got up and went back to the man
at the sign in table. He told the man at the
sign in table that he didn't think he wanted to
be an eagle anymore. The man at the sign in
table asked again, "what do you want to do,
what do you want to be?" About that time
Mr. Duck saw a rabbit running around the
track. That rabbit ran around the track so fast
that Mr. Duck said I want to be a rabbit and
run around the track. The man at the sign in
table said, "You know ducks don't make
good rabbits" but in life you get to make your
own choices, so the man at the sign in table
said, "Mr. Duck, have at it". Mr. Duck
started running around the track, but he
couldn't run too fast with those big webbed
feet he had. The rabbit made it around the
track two or three times before the duck made
it around once. Mr. Duck went back to the
man at the sign in table and said, "I don't
think I want to be a rabbit". The man at the
sign in table said, "well what do you want to
do, what do you want to be?" About that time

Mr. Duck saw a squirrel. That squirrel jumped from tree to tree to tree and from branch to branch to branch. Mr. Duck looked at the man at the sign in table and said, "I want to be a squirrel!" The man at the sign in table said, "You know ducks don't make good squirrels but have at it". Mr. Duck climbed the tree and jumped from one tree to the next but bang! He hit the branch and fell, boom! He hit another branch and fell. But this time when he fell, he fell into a pond. When he fell into the pond, Mr. Duck started treading water. When Mr. Duck started treading water everyone stopped in amazement of how well he treads water. The eagle with his great vision looked in awe. The rabbit stopped in mid stride (you know rabbits are afraid of water) to admire how well the duck tread water. He looked so calm, cool, and collective on top, but under the water he was peddling those feet with grace. He got out of the pond, went to the man at the sign in table, and said I don't want to be an eagle, I don't want to be a rabbit, and I don't want to be a squirrel. The man said, "Well what do you want to be?" He said a duck because that's what I do well!

You will never find happiness imitating someone else. Embrace who you are and your specific skillset. Here's an old proverb for you. If you is who you aint, then you aint who you is... And if you're not who you should be, you'll never be who you could be. Never settle for being an imitation of someone else, be the best you that you can be!

On a more personal note…

I was like most people from my neighborhood. I saw basketball or entertainment as the most likely way out. Growing up, my heroes were entertainers or athletes (we really have to introduce our kids to more role models). I'm not saying entertainers and athletes shouldn't be role models, but we do need them to see professionals represented. Anyway, I wasn't particularly good at athletics or entertainment. I was an average high school athlete at best and I couldn't carry a note across the street, so singing was out of the business. My big aha moment came when I joined the military and realized that people listened to me. I realized that I was really gifted in the areas of motivation and leadership. I noticed that people listened when I talked and oftentimes did what I asked, even when others couldn't get them to. I vividly remember situations while in the military, I was put in charge of soldiers that were not only older than I was, but they had more rank than I. The chain of command suggested they should be in charge, but my superiors would put me in charge. There were many times I was able to galvanize soldiers, encouraging them to work together on tasks they did not want to do. I remember asking myself at times "wow how'd you do that"? I also remembered the first time I remembered being a leader of men (although at the time I did not remember it). During a reflection, I remembered a particular wrestling practice during my junior year. My coach always leaned on the seniors to lead the team through conditioning drills. During this particular practice the seniors showed low energy (which was uncommon). Our coach got upset and told the seniors to get to the end of the line and asked me and a couple of other juniors to take the leadership roles. When I opened my mouth, there was an instant energy. The whole atmosphere changed, and the practice gained intensity. I didn't realize it then, but after reflecting on the event, I realized motivation and the leadership exhibited that day. As I reflected on my life, I realized areas of effectiveness. I recognized my gift.

Develop Good Friendships

"Who I hang around determines who I become"

The difference in where you are now and where you will be in 10 years is greatly affected by the people you hang around and the books you read. Are the people you hang around moving towards a worthwhile goal? Consider this, every moment you spend doing things that are of no value is time you forfeit that could be moving you towards your goal. I'm not suggesting every waking moment has to be spent moving towards your goal, but we have to be intentional in our effort to ensure we are constantly moving in the right direction.

I think one of the most difficult decisions young adults have to make is who to cut off and who to allow to continue to be in your circle of friends. There are people that you've known for a while, but you know they are not striving for greatness. As difficult as it may be, it is time to let them go. It is not that y'all don't have fun; it is that you are now striving for fulfillment. Listen, if they are not a friend of your tomorrow, they cannot be a friend of your today (Bishop John A. Tolbert, I). Now I'm not saying you must completely let go of everyone you know that's "finding" themselves, but I am saying that you can't let your time be consumed with people that aren't moving towards a worthwhile goal. Hanging around someone that's "finding" themselves won't help you find yourself. You'll actually lose yourself.

Success is free, but it does come with a cost. It will cost you friendships. Quite frankly, that's a price some aren't willing to pay. Well, they do pay for it. It costs their future. It costs their future children. It costs their dreams and goals. But at least they still have that friend... Wake up. You can't afford to waste time. While it's true that you have your whole life ahead of you, it's what you are doing now that's setting you up for your future success. If we aren't laying the groundwork for success, it won't happen. Success doesn't just happen. Success has less to do with intellect and ability and so much more to do with attitude and effort.

The time to start that hard work and dedication was yesterday. You need to develop good friendships because the time may come when you get discouraged and you need someone to get you back in gear. Again, you will get discouraged. You will get depressed. You do not need someone to tell you that it's okay to take a break or you don't have to work so hard. No. You need someone to tell you to stop feeling sorry for yourself, get up and get back to work. I live in Texas now, but I'm from Norfolk, Virginia. I lived across the street from the Atlantic

Ocean. My Texas friends like to fish, but when I was growing up, I preferred crabbing. I vividly remember catching crabs and putting them in a bucket to keep them until we got back to shore. When catching crabs, you don't have to put a lid on the bucket, because when one crab climbs up and tries to get out of the bucket, another crab will grab and pull him down. I tell you that story for two reasons. One is to encourage you to stay away from people who are like crabs in a bucket. Two is to discourage you from being a crab in someone else's bucket. Consider your relational involvements. Relationships can be classified in one of four categories:

Enemies- these are people that are open about their dislike for you. They don't mind telling people about your shortcomings and their desire to see you fail. Some are more subtle than others in that they may not be as vocal, but their desire to see you fail is the same. It is okay if someone doesn't like you. Wouldn't you rather know if a person didn't like you? At least you'd know where y'all stood.

Friends- these are the individuals that accept you the way they are. In my neighborhood growing up, I knew who my friends were because they had my back. They were the ones that were there when things got bad. They were the ones who I could depend on to pick me up when things got tough. They were friends. When I needed a ride or someone to spot me for a meal. These were the

individuals I looked to. We enjoyed each other's company and would sacrifice for each other.
A friend is someone that willingly gives you the right to take advantage of them. Because you are a good friend, you don't abuse that privilege. There is a mutual respect and appreciation for each other. So much so that years can pass by without seeing each other, but when you guys reconnect, it is as if you never left each other's presence.

Mentors- Friends accept you the way you are; mentors love you too much to leave you like that. Mentors are the ones that will tell you the things that you sometimes don't like to hear but it needs to be said. Parents, teachers, and spiritual leaders often fall into this category. That's why you sometimes experience that love/hate relationship with them. When things are going well, you love them, but when they catch you slipping and call you on it, there may be friction. Isn't it wonderful to have people in your life that love you enough that they don't mind upsetting you and being at odds with you for a season to tell you the things you really need to hear? If you have good mentors in your life, you should be extremely thankful. Mentors are important because they push you to reach heights of success that you might not attain without their persistent perceived pressure. Success is an interesting thing and often impossible to achieve without someone that pushes you when you feel like you can't go any further or sees the greatness in you that you don't see in yourself; so instead of hating on your mentors, appreciate them.

It's interesting how mentors are viewed over time. In the season of challenge, when mentors are pushing the hardest, the relationship may seem strained. As challenges and obstacles are overcome a mentor's influence and advice gains credit and appreciation. The length of time it takes you to identify and appreciate your mentors is directly related to your success. It's so easy to listen to your "friends" (frenemies), but face it, THEY AREN'T GOING ANYWHERE PRODUCTIVE! And they are trying to take you with them, to nowhere. Wake up! I'm not saying be mean, I'm saying put your future above that so called friendship. Tomorrow's success is far more important than today's fun/friendships. You can take my word for it today or live the experience tomorrow.

Frenemies- these relationships are the most difficult to navigate because of how you feel about the person. When you're around them, you have a really good time. There are a lot of positive attributes that you see in them. When you're around them, you feel good; however, you also notice that most of the trouble you get into is when you are around them. When around them there is a propensity to do things that could potentially damage your future. I know you like being around them, but again, at some point you have to make the decision that if you are not a friend of my future, you can't be my friend today. It's a difficult decision. A very mature decision... and a very essential decision. Many people have made life altering decisions because they listened to frenemies. Let me suggest you take a minute and reflect on the meaningful relationships in your life. Where do they fall? I also want you to identify the mentors in your life. Perhaps the person that purchased this book for you is a mentor. Do yourself and your mentor a favor. Call and tell them thank you. Also tell them what you've gotten from the book so far. After you do that I want you to think for a moment about how you and your mentors felt during and after the conversation. Isn't that awesome! The next step for you is to become a mentor for someone else by getting them this book. It can be found online. Have it mailed to them today!

I cannot leave this chapter without talking about the most important relationships you will have on earth. That is the relationship with your spouse (if you have one). How do you know if a particular person is the right one for you? That is an extremely good question. I can't say for sure that I can tell if they are the right one for you, but I do know that becoming the right person is as important as marrying the right person. If you begin by working on yourself (before you get married) and becoming a great spouse and your partner does the same thing, it will definitely make things easier. Let me give you this tidbit though. We are multidimensional beings. We are social, emotional, spiritual, financial, and intellectual. We need connections on all levels. It's important to find out if you are compatible/connected in these areas. You can tell by the answers to the following questions:

- Social- when something good happens to you, who are the first people you tell?
- Emotional- if something bad happens, who do you go to for comfort and support?
- Spiritual- who shares and supports your faith (whatever it may or may not be)?
- Financial- if you only had $100, who could get your last $100... Similarly, who do you know would give you their last $100? Also, who thinks the same as you about how to spend/save/invest money?
- Intellectual- who do you have stimulating conversations with concerning things that interest you?

Admittedly, most people I've given this little test to respond with a parent or sibling. That's a good thing because it means they have good familial relationships. I want to also suggest, when you can fill in the answers with a potential spouse, you may have a winner. When you find someone that you are compatible/connected with in these areas, then bring physical intimacy into the picture, it takes the experience to another level. It is more than having sex, it is making love!

Okay, enough of that... another personal story

The people I have surrounded myself with have greatly impacted my life. I'd go so far as to say that I wouldn't be here today without the people in my life. The first person of substantial influence in my adult life was SFC Sawyer. Unfortunately, he doesn't even know it. I stayed out too late one night while in the Army. I missed an important formation the next day and got into a lot of trouble. When I finally reported to duty, SFC Sawyer told me how much trouble I was in and that my particular squad had left for duty. He would have to drive me to my squad's location. While driving, he began talking to me about life. He began talking to me about what it meant to be a man and a soldier. I don't remember exactly what he said, but I'd imagined that fathers around the world often had talks like this with their sons. I can't explain how energized it made me feel. The next two gentlemen are the most important influences in my life. I became a Christian in 1994. My pastor was Lawrence Windom in Killeen Texas. He taught me how to be a man. He taught me how to be a husband. He taught me how to be a father. He didn't just talk to me but he modeled the behaviors that I needed to see. John Tolbert, who was my pastor while I was raising my children, is another such man. Not only was he my pastor, but he is my father-in-law (who you hang around really does determine who you become)! Without these men in my life, I'm not sure how different my life would be, but I do know it would be different.

Decide to Maintain a Positive Attitude

Attitude more so than aptitude ultimately determines altitude

The lion is known as the king of the jungle. Have you ever wondered why? The lion is not as big as an elephant, not as fast as a cheetah, nor as smart as a hyena. So why then is it king of the jungle? Attitude. The lion believes it is the king of the jungle. When the lion sees another animal, the lion thinks.. Lunch (Myles Munroe). Let me ask you a question, what do you do when you come face to face with conflict, fear, or challenge? What is your response? What is your attitude? Do you attack all obstacles with a can-do attitude? When things don't go your way, do you regroup and develop a better plan of attack?

I'm not saying you will always win but winning should always be your mentality. Let me dispel a myth about failure. Failure is not always a bad thing. Listen, the path to success goes through failure. Everyone fails! You can't quit simply because you encountered some obstacles! Henry Ford encountered many failures before he solidified the Model T Ford automobile. He said, "Failure is an opportunity to begin again, this time more intelligently."

What have you failed at recently? Why? Don't know, maybe it was your attitude. Maybe it was your effort. If you are lazy, undisciplined, hardheaded, and a know-it-all, you'll find it difficult to consistently succeed. OMG, I am so passionate about this topic... Okay let me slow down.

Successful people really do think differently. They are not better; they just think differently. They're not afraid to fail. Not afraid to lay it all on the line and have things not go their way. They are not paralyzed by someone saying no... by trying their best and coming up short. It's called life. Sometimes things don't go your way. Sometimes things are harder than you anticipated. Here's a suggestion for when things get hard. Try harder! Hard is not a bad thing. It's a reality of life. How you handle challenges has a huge impact on your overall success in life. It's not about being the smartest or having the highest IQ.

Do you have what is called GRIT? Can you keep a positive attitude in negative situations? Can you push beyond pressure? Here's the reality. The answer is not can you, it's will you. Nothing is too hard for you. Nothing is impossible. It's all about attitude and effort. I've never seen anything of great value be accomplished by low energy/negative individuals. Regardless if good things or bad things happen, always remember..Yesterday is history, tomorrow is a mystery. Today is a gift, which is why it is called the present. And if I want my tomorrow to be better than my today, I must do better today than I did yesterday. Because if I do today what I did yesterday, my tomorrow will be just like my today! I have to decide to maintain a positive attitude no matter the situation.

Let's look at how powerful the human brain (attitude) is. Your brain is so powerful that it can accomplish anything it's challenged to accomplish if the challenge is accompanied with diligence, positivity, and intelligent effort (the right attitude). You don't believe me do you? Consider this. No one ever thought a person could stay underwater for an extended period of time. No one ever thought you could go leagues under the sea and survive. Then John Philip Holland invented the submarine. No one ever thought man could fly; then the Wright brothers invented the airplane. No one ever thought man would travel outer space. Katherine Johnson's mathematical calculations of orbital mechanics eventually led to Neil Armstrong landing on the moon.

How did these events happen? People challenged their brains to solve these complex problems and guess what? The human brain did what it was challenged to do, because those individuals brought diligence, positivity, and intelligent effort. When faced with a difficult challenge,

instead of saying to yourself it can't be done,
ask yourself how it can be done. In doing so, you
challenge your brain to function on a greater
level. As explained in the examples above, when
the brain is challenged and supported with
tremendous attitude and effort, the results are
mind blowing. ` They accomplished great feats
because they challenged their potential in the face
of difficulty.

Far too many people tap out because it gets
difficult or hard. What really is hard? Hard does
not mean it can't be done. Hard doesn't mean
you can't do it. Oftentimes, hard simply means to
accomplish this task I will have to move out of
my comfort zone. The key to your ultimate
success in life is outside of your comfort zone.
Let me say that again. The key to your success is
outside of your comfort zone. The question is
not can you be great. You absolutely can, but
your greatness is outside of your comfort zone.
Think about an eagle in a storm. While other
birds are running for cover, do you know what
the eagle does? It rises above the storm. You can
rise above your proverbial storm.

What challenges are you facing? You can
absolutely overcome them. Listen, your ability is
not the issue. Your intelligence is not the issue. If
you bring diligence, positivity, and intelligent
effort, you can get through whatever challenge
comes your way and accomplish almost anything!
Let me take this a step farther. The key is not only

in having a positive attitude but maintaining a
positive attitude. Isn't it interesting how
mainstream thinking works against your success?
Mainstream thinking suggests it's okay to be
negative, condescending, and rude. Please bear
with this tangent I'm going on. Far too often I've
seen athletes quit if they don't get playing time,
band members quit because they are not first chair.
Let me help you. You're not the best at anything!
There is always someone better. The goal is not to
be the best. The goal is to be your best; to be the
best version of yourself that you can possibly be.
Life is a continual competition against yourself.
Are you better today than you were yesterday? That
should be your source of fulfillment, personal
growth.

Not being the best is not a reason to quit. It's
saddening that so many quit when things get
tough. Get thick skin. Life is tough, get
tougher. Listen, you'll never get anywhere
positive with a negative attitude. Show me
one person that lives a great life that has a
horrible attitude. They are few and far between.
It just doesn't work like that. Greatness begins
in the mind. It starts with a positive attitude.
Don't allow mainstream media to rob you of
this truth. Understanding this, I did research on
what successful people did to keep their
attitudes positive. I googled it. Yep, sure did, I
also read some books by some amazing
individuals. I found that many successful
people have a morning ritual that started them

off on the right track. How you start your day has a lot to do with how you finish your day. That's why it's important to start your day off right.

It's time to make the decision to begin starting each day off correctly. Remember, it's not just about making the decision to start your day off correctly. That decision has to be managed every day! There was one person's daily ritual that spoke to me, and I've embraced it and have benefited greatly from it. Tony Robbins is a business developer and life coach. In researching him (youtubing him) I stumbled on the power of priming. If you don't get anything else out of this chapter, get this. Before I tell you how I do it, I must admit that I didn't follow his exact prescription. If I were you, I'd google Tony Robbins priming to learn from the master.

Nonetheless, here's what I do. I get up (almost) every morning at 5am. I drink a glass of water and do a session of yoga or pilates. I've learned the benefits of this early morning stretch and/or core workout. Many muscular pains would be lessened through stretching, just as back pain would be reduced through a stronger core. Next, I sit in a quiet place and think of three things that I am proud that I've done or accomplished. I then think of three things that make me happy. I then open either my bible or notes I've taken from church service, speakers

I've listened to, or books I've read and go over them in my mind. Sometimes I'll get what I call a "word from God". I'm not trying to make you religious, but this has been my experience. I'll get an idea, a thought, or a challenge. If that happens, I pay close attention to it because I believe God speaks to me through his word. If you don't believe this, hey, do you, but it works for me. I'll meditate, ponder and think of the scriptures and strive to draw strength from them. I finish my priming session by thinking of 3-5 things I either want to do today or I don't want to do today.

For example, I had been "writing" this book for years. When I started writing this book in my priming sessions, it got written. I might say something like, I'm going to encourage someone today, or I am going to change my oil today. I will also say I am not going to let anger have any room in my life today. I am not going to give in to____________(the blank is a particular bad habit; you fill in your own) today. In doing so, I control the direction of my day. Starting your day off priming will tell your life what to do. No longer will life just happen to you. You will control your life, because you made a conscious decision to control your thoughts and your actions.

Do I always feel like doing this? Of course not. There has to come a point in time when we stop basing what we do on how we feel. The question is not **how** do I feel? The question is **what** do I need to accomplish today? There will be days when we have several tasks that we don't want to do. It's okay. We can still attack those tasks with a great attitude and give great effort. Now we're getting somewhere!

This seems like a good place to talk about enemies of your empowerment. Your empowerment is what will eventually lead you to success. Again, let me reiterate that you have everything you need to be successful. You have a unique blend of gifts, talents, and abilities that if capitalized on will lead to greatness. Let's talk about the enemies that will attempt to derail you. They are ignorance, apathy, and entertainment.

Ignorance- what you don't know can and will hurt you. If you apply the success principles that you are learning, you will undoubtedly achieve success. If you don't know these principles, you can't apply them. If you don't apply them, you won't reap the benefits of them. Don't get caught up in the myth of thinking all you have is all you need. There are things that you have not yet learned that will literally change your life. Similarly, there are things that you know conceptually, but haven't gotten them experientially yet that will change your world. That's why it is important to be a lifelong learner. Stay humble and stay open to new learning

Apathy- Personal growth doesn't just happen. We don't just learn more and get better. Personal and professional development both take intentional effort. To refuse to learn more is to refuse to get better. To refuse to get better is to stay where you are. I know you've accomplished some things to get where you are; however, you didn't get there to stop here. There is so much more that you can accomplish. This is not the time to get apathetic. This is not to time to stop learning, to stop growing, to stop getting better. When you're done growing... you're done.

Entertainment- A third enemy to your empowerment is entertainment. Far too many people spend far too much time watching TV, listening to music, watching movies, or surfing social media. Check your phone and see what activities are most common on your phone. If you spend most of your time on social media, watch you. You may be allowing today's entertainment to rob you of tomorrow's success. Please, I beg you.. don't let our media diet rob you of your greatness. Do this. Write down the specific steps you need take to reach your goals. Look at that list and tell me where social media is on that list. Tell me, where a large sports consumption is on that list. Tell me, where is a large reality television or an entertainment diet on that list. It's not. I'm not saying eliminate entertainment. We all need time to decompress and do things we find enjoyable. That is time well spent. You need to go to games and watch your favorite shows; however, if you're spending all night watching TV or surfing social media, you're wasting valuable time. It is time to set a limit on your entertainment diet. Discipline will determine your destiny.

Listen, untoward things will continue to happen to you. Don't allow that to determine your attitude. Your attitude had to be set like a thermostat. A thermometer will tell you the temperature, but a thermostat will set the temperature. It doesn't matter what's going on outside. It may be raining, snowing, or sunny and hot. The inside temperature is based on the thermostat. Similarly, it doesn't matter what's going on in your world, your internal thermostat says I will have a positive
attitude. A big part of maintaining this momentum is priming. It is as important as what/who you allow to influence you. This includes the people you're around, the music, television shows, and movies you listen to and watch. Conversations, television shows, and music all program us and help set our internal temperature. Often when a negative attitude is displayed, it is because we've allowed ourselves to be influenced by negative television shows, movies, lyrics, or frenemies. If you're typically a negative person, then you really need to watch your media diet...especially your social media diet, ijs. This my friends, is how you maintain

a positive attitude. I don't know about you, but I'm fired up!

Your influencers help shape your thinking. This in turn determines who/what is attracted to you. Just as mosquitoes are attracted to stagnant water and rodents are attracted to trash, who/what you are determines who/what you attract. If you are attracting the wrong types of things or people, it's time to change. Change what you attract, by changing the influencers in your life. As I close out this chapter, I'm reminded of what Colin Powell once said to me, "Perpetual optimism is a force multiplier." It's like a cold that's spread when someone sneezes and the whole room is infected. I challenge you to be a "cold" of optimism.

DISCLAIMER:

I have never met Colin Powell. When I listen to a speaker or read a book, I take the "conversation" personally. It is as if they are talking directly to me. They may not know the questions I have, but they have the answers I need, and they are sharing answers to the secrets of their success. Here's another personal story.

I read an article about Colin Powell, many

years ago. He made a statement that literally

changed my life. His said, "Perpetual

optimism is a force multiplier". In other

words, if you want to positively affect the "force", maintain a positive attitude. Life is a journey through ups and downs. It's easier to be positive in the up times. When you are up in the down times, you decrease the lengths of the downtimes because of your attitude. Your positive attitude will pull you out of a down season in your life. I remember watching a Los Angeles Lakers basketball game probably over two decades ago. The game sticks out in my mind because the Lakers where down by over 20 points in the first half. Instead of tucking their heads and accepting defeat, Pat Riley (coach of the Lakers) encouraged them to set small goals to get themselves back in the game. Instead of quitting because things seemed bad, they kept a good attitude, reestablished their game plan and eventually

won. You attitude has a lot to do with

your outcome.

Discern Life's Plan

There is something worse than death, that's being alive and not knowing why
> \- Myles Munroe

God's plan is less about what college you go to, what your job is, and what city you live in; it's more about who you become and what you do at that college, that job and that city- Steve Furtick

There is a reason you are here on earth. It's not simply to breathe air. You were born on purpose, for a purpose… God's plan is that purpose. I can almost hear some of you talking to yourself now, about how boring church is or how you plan on getting serious with God later in life. Listen, don't mistake God for church. Just because church is boring doesn't mean God is boring. Just because church is lifeless doesn't mean God is lifeless. I know sometimes church can almost put you to sleep; remember, God raised the dead!

It's sometimes difficult for church to seem relevant to some because you just don't relate to what's being said or the method of the services. Don't allow getting frustrated with church cause you to be frustrated with God. You may simply need to try another type of service or church. Listen; there is a church that has a message for you. The question is not, is there one out there, the question is have you found it. God has someone that speaks in such a way that it causes you to think about where you are in life, what you are doing with your life, and where you are going in your life. When you find that person, you've found your minister. When that person speaks, it's as if they are answering questions that you have but have never told them. It may not be the same person that you've listened to from childbirth. That's okay.

Acceptance of what you've just read will cause some family members to get mad at you, because some of you have been in a family church and some will say leaving that church is akin to leaving God. I respectfully disagree. Furthermore, when you find and follow your God given minister, you will experience freedom and joy like you've never experienced before. I apologize for the many churches that have done a disservice by not truly ministering to the needs of parishioners. Let me also suggest there comes a time when it's important to realize it's not so much about what I hear at church as it is about what I do with what I hear at church. There is a minister out there for you and there is a mission for you. You know you've found the right church when it pushes you towards your mission. A good question to ask is how can I serve others in, through, and with my church. If you can't come up with an answer, that may be the ultimate source of your disappointment. If the message being preached doesn't move you, you may be listening to the wrong message. I didn't say if the message doesn't challenge you or make you feel uncomfortable. The word of God will do that sometimes. The difference is it will be a message of conviction, not condemnation.

Conviction is when the word comes and you may feel bad, but you say to yourself, I have to do better, I can do better! Condemnation is when the word comes, and you feel beaten up and like you'll never get it together. Conviction says thank you God for helping me get it together. Condemnation says I'll never get it together. Anyway, the big thing is not so much what goes on in church. The bigger thing is what is going on in you. Furthermore, what's going on when you are out of church. What are you doing that's making a God-difference in your community? Are you volunteering, are you serving, wait are you simply being nice? What are you doing that's making a difference? Make no mistake about it God is calling you to make a difference. You may never have a worldwide ministry or even serve a high office in the church. That doesn't mean you're not making a difference.

You've probably heard the starfish story. A man and his son were walking along the beach talking. The tide had washed many starfish on the shore that were sure to die unless they quickly got back into the water. As the man was walking, he'd pick up

starfish and throw them back into the ocean.
His son said dad, there are way too many starfish
for you to throw them all back into the ocean, you're
wasting your time. You're not really making a
difference. The man picked up a starfish and said,
"To many of the starfish I'm not making a
difference but to this one (as he threw it back into
the ocean) I made all the difference in the world."
Similarly, most people are not called to influence
millions, but we are all called to influence many.
You may never have your name in lights, on
billboards, or on television. Nonetheless, your
impact is just as important to those that need it.

Simply put, there are people in your world that need
what you have to offer. Some may think, but I'm
not the supervisor or I'm not in charge. Influence
has less to do with position and more to do with
mentality. God's plan for you includes other people.
Let me ask you, how do you serve others? What is
it that you do that causes people to feel valued?
What is it that you do that causes people to smile,
to believe in themselves, to overcome obstacles?
For someone, it's preaching a sermon, or singing a
song. For others it's making sure the lighting and
sound is just perfect for the sermon or song. For
others, it's fixing a car, or cutting grass. Still for
others, it's that hug, kind word or smile. God has a
plan for us to impact others, and I encourage you to
talk to God to determine his plan for your life.

You've probably heard people say, or wondered
yourself, why is there so much lack and suffering in

the world? If God is in charge, why are things so bad? That's a good question. Consider this scenario. You have two cars. A close friend's car just died. Your friend desperately needs a car. Because you guys are so close, you tell your friend I just got a tune up and new tires on this car and I'm going to let you drive it as long as you need it. About a year later your friend comes back and throws you the keys. She informs you that the tires on your car are bald and it won't start anymore. Whose fault is it? The car does belong to you, but you allowed your friend to control the usage of the car. Similarly, God gave man dominion over the earth. The earth is in its condition not because God failed, but because man failed. Men did not follow the plan of God for their lives causing people to go lacking. When people go lacking, society fails.

Everyone doesn't need what you have to offer, but there are people that most assuredly do. Identify those you are called to bless and begin doing so. Identify what you have to offer to the world and begin doing so. Identify God's plan for your life and start walking in it. International business consultant Myles Monroe made a great point when he said "purpose proceeds production." Let me explain, companies do not produce products, and then wonder what to do with them. The purpose for the product is established then the production comes. Metaphorically speaking it is difficult for you to be productive or meet your maximum level of productivity if you don't know your purpose. You know you are discovering your purpose when you begin to become uncomfortable with your norm. When you start realizing you have to do something different. It's not necessarily something more or better, it's just something different. For someone it's going back to school. For someone else, it is stepping down from a time intensive job to do something else. It is your purpose, and you need to find it!

Your purpose is your preset plan. Purpose is what gives you the drive, so let me ask what are you driven to do? If the answer is I don't know that's okay. Look at the opportunities you have and start taking advantage of them and see what sparks your interest. It may not initially spark your interest, but the more you get involved, the more interested or motivated you get. If you're still unsure, just start doing things. Start working at different things and see what piques your interest. See what you are naturally drawn to. Try a lot of things. Volunteer and become a lover of learning. As you continue to challenge and develop yourself, you'll find your passion.

This is very important. If you are not a person of faith, I suggest you skip over this section, but I have to reiterate this. It bothers me, the number of people that are turned off by church or God because of the way Christianity was presented to you. Just because your church was a dead church that didn't understand how to minister to you, doesn't mean the gospel is boring. Just because you were made to go to church because of family ties doesn't mean

the gospel isn't for you. The way it was presented
to you may have been boring, but the gospel is not
boring. Christ is not boring. Salvation is not boring.
Trust me it's the way the gospel was presented
and/or your mentality towards its value. Think
about it like school. How many boring classes have
you had that you hated attending? But... do you
remember the other teacher that made you enjoy
going to class and learning?

Some churches are like the first teacher. The class
you hated attending. You needed the information,
but you hated the class. When you appreciated the
teacher and the class, it became much better. It is
important to find that church that's like the second
scenario. The one that made learning fun and
meaningful. They are out there. If you can't find
one in your area, maybe it's because God wants you
to help start one. You know what kids go through
and you could make a youth group meaningful
and relevant, so why not do it. Maybe you
understand divorce, or depression, or being
abandoned and can explain to others how to recover
from a desperate situation. It may be that you're
so frustrated with church because God is calling
you to change church as we know it. Why not make
a meaningful difference?

Listen, life is about a whole lot more than going to
the next party or the club on the flyer. Get a grip! If
that's where you are and what you're about, do us
both a favor and put this book down! No, give it
away to someone that gets it! It's time to grow up.

Maturity is not about doing what you want to do.
It's about doing what you should do. It doesn't
mean you don't listen to anyone; it means you've
finally figured out who you should be listening to.
If you're still reading, then this is for you. Not
because you're better than anyone else, but because
you've figured it out. It's not simply about making
the plan it's about managing the plan. Success in life
is not about who's smarter, more athletic, or better.
It's about who figures out the formula for success.
It's about who implements successful strategies on
a daily basis. It's about discipline.

Discipline Yourself

You will become what you are becoming

In the book Great by Choice, Jim Collins explains the importance of fanatical discipline. Discipline requires consistency. It is the consistency of actions in accordance with goals and values over time that yields desired results. Jim suggests a key to success is consistency over time. Again, it all goes back to attitude. Attitude more so than aptitude, ultimately determines altitude. If we continually do the things that lead to success, we can overcome any shortcoming.

Many through college have learned (and many of you about to go to college will learn), early failure isn't final. Many students are not as successful as they'd like to be during their first semesters in college. They are too lazy, undisciplined, and immature. They had to learn the importance of paying attention in class regularly, studying regularly, and consistently overcoming emotional, physical (hunger), and monetary setbacks. They had to learn discipline. It is not always easy to be a college student and only the disciplined survive. Discipline suggests a person continues to do what it takes to be great. I've learned that discipline, attitude, and effort are much more important than intellect, ability, and IQ.

Continue learning, continue growing, continue listening to peers and mentors, and continue reading.

As I've studied many successful people, I've learned they've turned their cars into Automobile University. Automobile University is when you cut the music off in your car and listen to podcasts or messages of men and women that challenge and direct you on how to identify your potentials and fulfill your passions. Listen, the question is not can you be great. You can be great. But greatness is not a function of circumstances. It's a function of conscious choice and discipline - attitude and effort. Again, you can be great. The question is will you consistently display the right attitude and effort.

A key component of discipline is focus. Consider this water is not a threat to society unless it's focused. It's actually welcomed. People take vacations to the beach, pay to go to water parks, and play in the rain. Yet when water is focused, it can become a hurricane or a tsunami that creates tremendous problems. Consider sunlight. We conduct most of our daily activities while the sun is out. Some even lay out in the sun, but when light is focused, it can produce a laser beam that can cut through steel. Focused discipline exponentially increases your effectiveness and impact. The question is not can you get to the next level, the question is will you do what it takes to succeed.

One more analogy, then a couple of examples.
Consider the eagle. Perhaps the most majestic
bird known to man. So much so that the United
States has made it the national bird. An
interesting note about the eagle is how it
handle's storms.

Eagles don't handle storms like most birds. Most
birds run for cover when they find themselves in a
storm. The eagle on the other hands spreads its
wings and rises above the storm. Disappointments
and challenging times will come. Discipline
yourself to maintain daily discipline in the midst of
the madness. There's really no way around it.
Heartache and disappointment will come but
remember this. In the midst of despair, double
your determination to succeed (Bishop A.L.
Thomas, Sr.). We all face tough times, but
yesterday is history, tomorrow is a mystery. Today
is a gift which is why it is called the present. If I
want my tomorrow to be better than my today, I
must do something different today than I did
yesterday. Because if I do today what I did
yesterday, my tomorrow will be just like my
today!

It's daily discipline that leads to destiny. It is the
daily choices I make, not chance that
determines whether I reach my destiny or not.
Just as discipline is a key to success, almost all
failure can be traced back to a lack of self-
discipline. A lack of self-discipline leads to
failure, frustration, underachievement, and

unhappiness. Success is not about how smart you are, how talented you are, or how lucky you are. Those things are important and are definitely useful, but there is something that matters more. You know what matters more, how disciplined you are. Undisciplined people are very good at making excuses. Be wary of excuses, as they are often attempts to reestablish the norm or expectation at a lower level.

Set a goal and begin to exercise daily disciplines that will lead you to reach that goal. Daily discipline determines destiny. What are you doing every day that is leading you towards the goals you've set for yourself? How are you marketing, learning, developing, and growing every day? There is no substitute for hard work! Have you ever heard about the elephant, the jumping flea, and the piranha? You gotta hear this. The next time you go to a circus, try to go behind the curtains to where the animals are kept. It's interesting that the baby elephants are held to the stake by a huge chain, but the adult elephants are held with a rope. I thought to myself, why would they use a huge chain to hold the baby elephants, but a small rope to hold the adult elephants. Then I realized why. The baby elephants are constantly trying to escape, so they use the huge chain. The adult elephants remember the many times they tried to escape as babies. It never worked, so now they have stopped trying. Isn't it something that if the adult elephant tried one more time, it would break free?

If you consider the size of the jumping flea and compare it to the height it jumps, the ratio is as high as any other organism on earth. Some jumping fleas were put in a box and a lid was put on the box. The jumping fleas tried to jump out of the box but boom. They hit their heads on the top of the box. They tried this for two weeks and every time they tried, they hit their heads. The third week, the top was taken off of the box, but the jumping fleas remembered hitting the top of the box, so they didn't even try. Isn't it something, that if they would have tried one more time, they would have jumped out of the box? A piranha was placed in a tank. On the other side of the tank were placed a few goldfish. In between the piranha and the goldfish was placed a clear plate of glass. The piranha saw the goldfish and made a beeline for them and wham! Ran right into the glass. The next day the same thing was done. The piranha again made a beeline for the goldfish and again, wham! It ran into the clear plate of glass. The third day, they put the piranha on one side, the goldfish on the other, but they didn't put the plate of glass in the middle. The piranha remembered failing the first two times, so this time, the piranha didn't even try. Isn't it something, that if the piranha tried one more time, it would have gotten to the goldfish. Discipline is the mentality to keep on even in the face of presumed failure. Discipline will oftentimes take you further that intellect will. Don't quit because it's hard, don't quit because you can't figure it out. Take the word quit out of your vocabulary. You don't quit until you've either accomplished your goal or you're dead. It's just that simple. Maintain the discipline to see it through till the end!

As I close this book with final thoughts, I want to remind you that this is not an all-inclusive book. This book is not intended as a be all end all. It is simply the next steps to take in your success journey. I encourage you to develop financial literacy and health awareness as well. It is important to know the difference between asset and liability. It is important to know the difference in earned income, passive income, and portfolio income. It is important to start a business and learn tax advantages. As an example, consider the professional athletes that surrender upwards of 40-50% of contractual earnings in taxes if uneducated.

Here's an example of an athlete whose
gross pay is $33M $33,200,000 gross pay
- $3,200,000 escrow (10%)

-11,900,000 federal income taxes

-$2,100,000 city/state taxes

-$ 950,000 agent fee (often 3%)

-$ 18,000 401(k) savings

+$1,600,000 returned escrow from prior year

+$ 188,000 sport revenue split

$16,820,000 take home pay

Is this eye opening or what! The athlete signed a
$33M contract, yet the take home pay is almost
half. People wonder why athletes go broke. Two
reasons. Number one, they spend the amount they
signed for, but only see the take home pay. Number
two they don't understand how to reduce the
amount they pay in taxes. Some might say, but I'm
not a professional athlete. The tax system is not
much better to salaried employees. Learning how to
properly negotiate the tax system will save money.
Not just for the highly compensated professional
athletes, but also for the average person on an
hourly wage or a yearly salary.

Another important component of your success is
your health awareness, both physically and
mentally. It is important to maintain both physical
and mental health. It is possible that some
undiagnosed illnesses can be linked to dehydration,
poor diet, and poor mental health. The same is true

with poor relationships. They can be exacerbated by an unhealthy mental outlook.

My desire is that after reading this book, you are ready to conquer the next phase of life. Hit me up and let me know how things are going. Drltcollins18@gmail.com.

Review of the 5 areas and key phrases:

1. <u>Discover Your Strengths</u>- Understand your unique blend of gifts, talents, and abilities
If you is who you aint, then you aint who you is... and if you're not who you should be, you'll never be who you could be-- old proverb

2. <u>Develop Good Friendships</u>- Who you hang around determines who you become
Who I hang around determines who I become

3. <u>Decide to Maintain a Positive Attitude</u>- Attitude moresoe than aptitude ultimately determines altitude *Attitude moresoe aptitude ultimately determines altitude*

4. <u>Discipline Yourself</u>- You will become what you are becoming
You will become what you are becoming

5. <u>Discern Life's Plan</u>- No one can do what you
have been called to do. If you don't do it,
the world will go lacking.
There is something worse than death, that's being alive and not knowing why- Myles Munroe

It's time to take your next steps towards significance...

NOW GO BE GREAT!